Usborne
First Sticker Book
Dinosaurs

Illustrated by Jordan Wray

Words by Hannah Watson
Designed by Keith Newell

Contents

With expert advice from Ed Drewitt

You'll find all the stickers at the back of the book.

Munching leaves

Stick on some more long-necked Diplodocuses and hungry Stegosauruses grazing on plants and trees. Plant-eaters like these are called herbivores.

Diplodocus

Stegosaurus

Hatching eggs

This Maiasaura is guarding her nest from Bambiraptors who are waiting to pounce. Maiasaura means 'good mother lizard'. Stick on some more parents and some little babies who have already hatched.

Bambiraptor

Maiasaura

T-rex attack!

Some scientists now think that the Tyrannosaurus rex had feathers. This fierce T-rex has spotted a Triceratops for lunch! Stick on lots more dinosaurs running away.

Triceratops

T-rex

In a swamp

Edmontosauruses lived in warm, tropical swamps. Stick on some more dinosaurs, and some bright flowers. Fill the water with turtles and fish.

Edmontosaurus

Spotted turtle

Lepisosteus

Under the sea

Ichthyosaurs and plesiosaurs lived in the ocean, along with spiral-shaped ammonites and lots of prehistoric fish. Add them all to this tropical scene.

Dapedium

Pholidophorus

Ichthyosaurus

Plesiosaurus

In the air

The wings of the enormous Quetzalcoatlus were as wide as a small plane. Fill the sky with these amazing flying creatures and add another nest of eggs to the clifftop.

By the coast

Scelidosauruses roam this rocky coastline looking for plants to eat, while Dimorphodons fly overhead. Add more of these to the picture and fill the water with sea creatures.

Dimorphodon

Scelidosaurus

More dinosaurs

Find all of the dinosaur stickers to match these shapes
and labels. How many do you recognize?

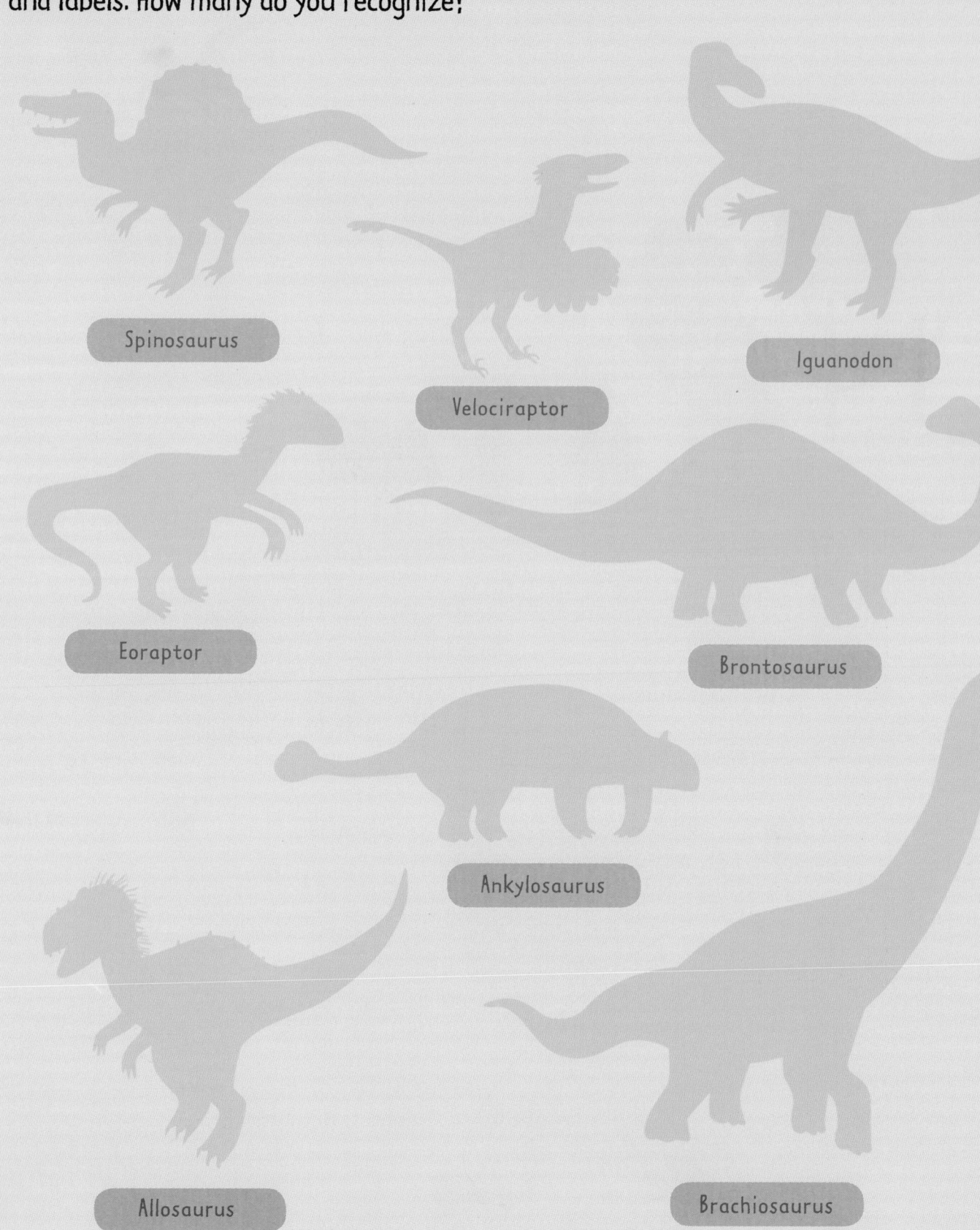

Spinosaurus

Velociraptor

Iguanodon

Eoraptor

Brontosaurus

Ankylosaurus

Allosaurus

Brachiosaurus

Munching leaves

Diplodocus

Stegosaurus

Hatching eggs pages 4–5

Maiasaura

Maiasaura nest

Bambiraptor

T-rex attack! pages 6-7

Pachycephalosaurus

Struthiomimus

T-rex

Triceratops

Lepisosteus

Spotted turtle

Edmontosaurus

Amia

Under the sea pages 10–11

Plesiosaurus

Ichthyosaurus

Ammonite

Pholidophorus

Dapedium

Quetzalcoatlus

Quetzalcoatlus nest

By the coast pages 14–15

Dimorphodon

Scelidosaurus

Pholidophorus

Ammonite

Dapedium

More dinosaurs page 16

page 16

Allosaurus

Brachiosaurus

Ankylosaurus

Brontosaurus

Iguanodon

Spinosaurus

Eoraptor

Velociraptor

You can use these stickers anywhere in the book.